FONG MIN LIAO

THROUGH THE VEINS OF MY HEART

ISBN 9798218124601

I have learned the art of dying. To bring death upon the women who had once lived within me. It is their deaths that give birth to the woman I am today. As one cannot truly live unless one is intimate with death. I must change in form if I desire to grow and to outgrow who I once was. Because who I am tomorrow will no longer be who I am today. And it is foolish to think that who you were yesterday can claim the gifts that belong to who you are tomorrow.

This is for you, my dearest reader.
Thank you for being here.

The process of falling in love with myself and the
lovers who touched my heart in between.

Marked By The Color Red

A part of me is on the brink
of death, as I stand on this cliff's edge
I face her, I hold her hand and I whisper,

> thank you for protecting me,
> thank you for nurturing me.

It is time for you to now go
and she knows, that I must find
my new flow.
On this journey I once again embark alone,
the flames begin and I watch her burn,
I held on 'til the very last flame singed
my fingers.

It began in my chest, the burning
sensation that felt so familiar
she is another chapter that is now embedded
in my figure.

And so I am reborn
enveloped in the color red.
A part of me I have shed, with blood I bled.
I won't mourn, but rather rejoice
because it is my choice.

To begin this life anew, a desire
for a breakthrough
to expand my world views.

The memories visit
every now and then, I see
in my mind's eye and feel the emotions
within.
How bittersweet it can be
what once was, is no longer here with me.
But I have been reborn,
marked by the color red
it represents this very life I have lead.

Emotional and vulnerable, a young woman
I am.
I live this life with my passion, my tears,
with my heart torn
because it is on this life I have sworn,
to be an expression of my purest individuality,
to embrace all my dualities.

So I am reborn
marked by the color red.

From The Ashes Of My Death

I have died over and over,
engulfed in flames
burning my flesh and soul
pain and anguish that swallows me whole.

Rebirth, she said
is your soul's journey that you must honor
and respect.

Each experience is a nutrient
every emotion, a medium
to form the blueprint that runs through your veins
a timeline that will transcend your pain.

So I rise from my ashes,
I let go of what I saw as tragic,
I embody my new being
at once I see

how this frees me.

Unfolding

On the floor weeping
clutching my chest, afraid to let go
with fear that if I do,
I would crumble.
I knew
            it was time

to tell my story.

Because if I did not,
it would absorb my entire
being,
leaving me to wilt.

I now know
there are stories that live within us
and there are stories

living
            beyond us.

My Rising

I do not know how to not feel
as I do, a passionate person who feels too deeply,
loves too much and cares more
than I should.

This is who I am,
no desire to be any different,
never trading my heartbreak
for a heart unwounded.

I will not stay in silence
for I have too much to express,
not abide by the rules made to suppress,
not be confined nor conditioned,
I will not be made small.

My north star, the inner light I lead this life with
all the sorrows, burdens and heartbreaks
flow through me to be washed
away, nourishing me with wisdom
knowledge,
through pain one learns
how to rise.

Like a phoenix I will burn, and continue to burn
as many times as I need to, to unlearn
and relearn
        what it means to be a being
with values rooted in love
not hatred, for this life
        was not meant to be limited.

Stories

So many stories living
within me,
dying to be born,
but how do I
embrace
the paradox that I am
when this world
only desires

everything

that I am not.

Precious Words

My words, always spoken
the golden threads
keeping me together,
stitched by hand
one by one with unwavering love
casting away the pain
I desired to be free of.

So desperate was my aim
gathering each word, spilled
pieces of grain,
kneeling on the floor,
hands in prayer
whispering,
hoping the eternal being would hear.

Cries to piercing screams,
tears falling in streams,
I could no longer hold it in,
this burning pain

       was more than I could bear.

Bloodline

Remembering now who I used to be
who I am today, who I am to become.
My duty to protect
the traditions around me,
the heritage rooted within.

I will not waver for I am the daughter
of the blood that runs through my veins,
giving my promise to always be true,
I will not have endured in vain.

Like water, I flow softly
but do not mistake my yielding
a weakness,
for it is water
            that wears away rock.

Phoenix

With the spirit of her ancestors,
she finds the courage
to shake
the ashes
of what once burned
from her wings.

Storing over a thousand
years of secrets and sorrows
in her heart,
she takes flight.

Awakening

There I was,
floating
between the worlds of conscious
and unconscious.
My throat felt tight,
hard to breathe.
I could feel the air
slowly seep
out of my lungs
leaving me.

Forbidden Territory

My heart, closed,
is a place of history
its walls and ceiling drenched
in memories.

My heart, open,
is a place
of possibilities
a home ready,
for new beginnings.

Rewritten

No longer a victim
of my past, no longer compromising
boundaries.
Shedding old skins,
washing away my sins,
my soul and essence unfolds
with each page,
ink to paper, I am water
carving a new path in these mountains,
flowing steadily with a gentle force
I am finally home,

      home to myself.

Manifesting

After endless searching,
I truly see the power of creation,
and you and I,
there is no separation.

It only exists as an illusion of desperation,
for I know now, that all I desire
all that I wish for
is already mine,
as long as it is spoken for.

To remember who I truly am
to remember my being
I make way, for the woman I wish to become
for she has always been within
and I am ready

to give in.

Faith Is My Fortune

I knelt on my knees in prayer
to him, the inner being within,
they say "ask and you shall receive"
I earnestly wished for some relief.

I surrender my trust in you,
it is then I realize my breakthrough
him and I are one,
all previous beliefs come undone.

I discover the real kingdom of heaven
all things are possible
                        at the hour of eleven,
persisting with determination,
no matter how long the duration.

For You

Dare
to do what is right
          for you,
even if others do not understand
even if the whole world says you can't
even if it does not make any logical sense
          in the eyes of others
even if your surroundings are devoid of life,

you can bring your own colors.

Learning

The beautiful thing about love and loss
are the lessons you will come across.
To learn how to love and to grieve,
knowing when to stay, when to leave.

To transcend and to transform
that has always been my goal.

We live with a duality within us,
an ebb and flow of yin and yang,
finding balance between pleasure and pain.

Rose Tinted Eyes

My unwavering persistence of pushing through
exists only because of my desires,
a desire to fully exist in being,
a desire to live surrounded by beauty,
but a beauty that only I can see
        perhaps one day you will join me.

Her Death Gave Birth To Me

I felt my old self dying,
the pain of my shedding,
I had to let her die.
Softly,
melting into my embrace.
To be reborn,
her skin
was set on fire.

Deepest Yearnings

I wanted nothing
more than to be able to express
how I felt,

the way
my heart sung,

the way
my heart hurt.

The Beauty Of Emptiness

There is a joy,
finding pleasure
in the simplest
things.

It begins
with emptying our minds,
our hearts.

So that we may fill
again with the possibilities
that we once
could not see.

Bloom

To bloom into being,
from darkness to light,
because it is my open wounds
that fueled my vision and sight.

Her Seasons

The seasons changed
came spring and summer
like a flower,
she blossomed
her petals gently curled outward
the delicate curves of her pleats,
        she knew it was her time.

Phasing

A new moon
a turning point
winter solstice upon the horizon,
let me dwell in softness and upon awakening,
I will once again bloom.

Because this is a time
        for blossoming,
        this is my time of becoming.

Unbearable Soul

I refuse to live in denial
to be clothed in lies
and half told truths.
I desire
to be naked in who I am,
secrets buried in my heart,
to bare my soul
for those who can see
beyond
             their senses.

Promise

I see her
for the first time in my life
raw and vulnerable, cut open with a knife
wielded by my very own hand,
it was time to expand.

I watched my old skin shed
layer by layer it bled,
demanding self-respect.

Moving forward,
this is the only way
when the days are hard,
when the days are long,
a desire to transcend
it shall be
because this desire
            is a promise

made to me.

Like Moon, Like Daughter

Just as the moon
waxes and wanes in its perfect timing,
I too,
embrace my own life
with its yin and yang.

My 1,000th Rose Bud

A thousand deaths so I can be reborn
to see this world with new wings,
this thorned rose will not mourn
for she knows the presents life brings.

Patience Is A Virtue

Even if my heart
shattered
into the finest glass shards
I will pick up the pieces, one by one.

Healing takes time
I will nurture this wound
for I know, liberation
will be mine.

Mother Nature

There are stories
within us
like a river, flowing from east to west.
Our past blends
into our present,
thus our future.

It is in vain
to stand against the currents
of our fates
because it is through our seasons,

winter,
spring,
summer,
autumn,

that our lives take shape.

Existential Crisis

I write because my heart
needs to, the words bleed
from my veins and weep
from my eyes, leaving
stories
            that are my soul's cries.

See Me In Your Eyes

The silence was deafening,

a stillness,
that shook the earth.

Unraveling

I want to be seen
in my rage
my anger, and my twisted pain.

The processes of blossoming,
withering,
embrace me

in all my messy,

open-hearted

truths.

Breakdown To Breakthrough

I burned and burned, my self
to be a light for others
now, I will burn, to be the light for me
and from my ashes,
the truth can be seen from my eyes.

Authenticity

Being a woman, and what it means
I am only learning
the truth of that now.
In love
with what I am discovering,
what I am remembering.

This world is a sensual one,
and I commit
to only living in ecstasy,
living in love.

Because I see
no other way of being,
except to be our fullest
and most authentic

selves.

There Was Never A Time I Was Ready

The memories I held on for so long
it was time to let them go,
no longer places to revisit
rather moments to remember.

The Power In You

Everything is a reflection
what you seek is within
believe
and you shall see
your decision, your beliefs

know it into being.

Drifting Thoughts

The air sung to me
like wind chimes of spring
how sweet the sound,
how lovely it felt.

Another time
another place,
memories so fleeting
but feelings so vivid.

Seedling

I am my own flower
that I must nourish with sun and water
but most of all, I need the deepest fertile soil
and that first begins
within.

26th Year

How was I supposed to know
what it means to be this woman,
I am
sweet innocence
no longer
for she has grown
and all she has ever known

shattered

to pieces of delusion.

Lilith

Dark and filled with fire,
men's weaknesses she inspires,
worshipped at her feet
her scent musky and sweet.

Gaze so piercing,
a sinner birthing,
goddess of the black moon,
siren in love with her own tune.

Dancing in the shadows,
moonlight worn like lingerie,
angel of the night.

She can hear your soul's call,
there when you take your first breath,
there when you reach your death.

Whispering in your ear
her voice quells your heart's fear,
to her you wish to surrender,
to show how much

you desire
        her.

Painted In Her Mind

Her skin soft as silk
every curve and angle caressed
by the warm embrace
of him,
filled to the brim,
her heart,
true,
deep red and blue.

Alive In Her Light

The moon in her
shines
on your darkest
deepest secrets.

Her desire
a red that burns
so brightly like molten
lava, filled with sins
and sorrows,

       only a sliver is shown.

Ode To You, My Flower Bud

My sweet flower,
how you bloom so beautifully
rising above the ground,
your earthy scent
nourishing my heart,
your petals softly spreading apart,
a silent beauty that is so precious

like a dream in blossom.

Worship

The art of being a woman,
the dance between lover and friend,
the delicate balance of the sensual sweet spot,
a brazen statement with a seductive eye,

you blink once

and she's gone.

Possibilities

Be deaf

when the world tells you to contain
your dreams,

be blind

when the world
tells you that you are not beautiful.

Know that within your heart,
you are indeed the most beautiful,
know that within your mind,

anything

is possible.

She

The feminine essence
longs to be free,
to be unchained,
wild.
She is within
dancing
together until we are one,
her seduction
entrances me
and I am pulled into the deep.
I surrender
in her vast ocean,
emerging anew.
For she is I

and I am

her.

Lost Child

The pain in my heart,
an ancient map
guiding
back to the inner child
who only desired to be loved,

to be cherished,

held.

Melancholy

The days I dwelled
in sadness
much like my childhood
lullabies, familiar tunes
sun setting afternoons
I said goodbye,

too soon.

Sacred Unearthing

The blessing
in disguise
was finding
who I have become
in
solitude.

Mine

I thrived
in my own secret little worlds.
They were mine

and mine only.

Darkness, My Goddess

No longer afraid,
finding my home in the dark,
she welcomed me,
embraced me,
became my solace.

Heartquake Of The Century

I became the love I never received
and through it all,
the most beautiful gift

was that it
finally

set me free.

I Must Go Where I Feel Most Alive

I yearned
so deeply to be free,
a freedom
I craved so immensely,
to be free as I please,
          as wild as I desire.

Only For This Moment

My eyes filled
with the color red
the color
that leaves me wanting more,
furiously in love,
mesmerizing,
the warmth of her wetness
sweat on her brow
          air thick with desire.

Seduced

Show me the tenderness
within, my chaos and my calm,
you were
a never-ending love affair.

Alive

I let him enter me
in all my vulnerability.

My Private Garden

I want pleasure and I want bliss
so come closer, give me a kiss,
to lose myself in you
to immerse my soul in all that you do,
for you
        have pulled my heart strings.

Your hand,
the warmest I ever felt,
my cold dark heart,
        it melts.

Revealing the deep red within,
unveiling the new me I would begin.

My private garden,
only privy to you,
little seedlings once sown
        now grown
stems of red, burgundy and pink.

A Heaven's Love

You dissolve my pain,
your love on me like showers of rain,
let me take you to heaven,
on me you've left a lasting impression,
be my sun, my clouds
        and I, your moon, your stars.

That One Spring Night

The night I met you,
I felt my heart resurrecting,
finally beating,
blood pumping,
the oxygen
bursting
through my veins.

I wanted to sink
into your body,
to merge with your being.
I wanted you to devour
me,
for you to find my flavors,
to discover my textures.

I craved nothing more
than to feel
your lips
against

mine.

Sonder

You were a new possibility
that alone excited me,
when I see you, electricity
runs through my body,
charging
me, in ways

I have never felt before.

The Dream

I want to love,
deeply love,
to meet you at the depths
of our souls.

I want to feel
as expansive as the sky,
going on for eternity, infinitely.
            Is a love
like this possible?, my heart asks.

How I desire to love

a love
            without boundaries.

The Desire

I wanted him
to seduce my mind
with the same passion
as his passionate heart.
I wanted
to be
the sun
of his universe.

When I Saw You

I passed by you
as you brushed against me,
it felt as though time
stopped
for us to see.

Eyes nearly meeting,
mouths nearly speaking,
trapped in mind and thoughts,
interactions,

interrupted.

Merging

What shall I do,

if I were to fall in love with you,
all I see is your beautiful face
wrapped up in a warm embrace.

I breathe into you as you breathe into me
it is when we are together,
that my heart feels complete.
I do not know nor can I see
            what the future holds,
but this right here is where I want

to be.

My Love

When I look at you,
I am at a loss of what to do,
for you have me under a spell
for you my soul I would sell.

The moment I met you, I knew
that you were the one who I would come to
you made space for me,
allowed for us to be.

Daring to dive deep into the depths
no matter how many steps or breaths
to give life to our love
because you are all I can think of.

I want nothing more
than to be by your side,
to build a life with you

is all I want to do.

Lotus In The Mud

Take me, absorb me
tell you love me
if you say yes, I can be your heaven
I can be a saint even with my sins
or I can be the sinner in your hell,
keep my secrets
because I only show,
not tell.

This Moment Together

Light caresses sending shivers
down my spine,
our arms and legs intertwine,
my back arches
underneath your touch,
I didn't know
I'd crave you this much,
your kisses are my addiction,
at mercy for your affection.

Under the moonlight, I see
your silhouette,
a vision
I will never forget.

You make me laugh
with your silly jokes,
make me surrender
with your soft strokes,
it feels so safe
to be in your arms,
always seducing
with your charms.

Taking my breath away,
I think to myself how I
have never felt this way,
every second I waited
for you felt like a day,

I imagine what I would say.

Siren's Love

I was his dark moon
singing the song of his heart's tune,
his brightest star
the greatest love of his by far,
only I knew
what to do,

what he needs,
what he desires.

I was his wildfire
burning down his heart's walls,
his ego's downfall,
it was I that he belonged with,
our love already
written
in heaven's myth.

The Warmth Of Red

Wrap me in your red,
for once all is done and said,
it is the raw and the real that matters
and it is this red.

I desire nothing more than to love,
of my own shadows that I would be free of,
haunted by this yearning,
deep in my heart it is returning.

By Your Side

I want to be your wild girl,
a man who understands my gifts,
love me deep, love me sincere
with you
I am willing to go anywhere.

Taste

I loved the way you opened my flower gently,
the way you dipped your finger in my honey,
you said you wanted to taste me,
I said, yes please.
So hold me fast and hold me tight,
because I have never felt so right.

Burning Desire

I have this deep burning desire within
to lose myself in intoxication,
in a love so deep I will be shaken to my core
to be stripped naked for you to explore.

I have this deep burning desire for you,
to be reawakened in a way that only you knew
to be carried to the doors of heaven
in your arms, in your possession.

I have this deep burning desire, it's true
the only one in this world I want is you
can you see me in my truth
let my love be your fountain of youth.

So take me now, take me here
my burning desire is for you, my dear.

I Don't Want Surface Level

I want to swim
in the deepest depths,
unafraid to dive
into the black abyss.

I am greedy, I said.
I want a love that burns
a luscious flame,
passionately,
intoxicating,
because this is who I am
and that is how I love.

I watched you watching me,
your eyes move
from my crown to my feet.

If I were to tell you
the truth of who I am
would you still
accept me with all that I am?

My heart, in all its vulnerability
the darkest of nights
a life of bliss, surrounded by beauty
everything the eye can see,
can have its own artistry.

Fasten Your Body To Mine

Skin to skin
yours against mine, setting
fires blazing,
your touch leaving trails
of smoke swirling,

I breathe in your scent
and you, mine

musky,
earthy,

sweet.

My Selcouth Soul Isn't Just For Anyone

Beautiful,
violent and vulgar,
that is the description of my heart,
coloring of my soul.

One who understands my depths
could only see
the gifts I could give
overflowing.

Euphoria

I decided I would love
and love with the fierceness
and chaos
of my heart.

Basorexia

That sweet taste
of the first kiss.
I wanted tenderness,
wildness.
I wanted love
and lust. I wanted to become
that which I could only be
when I am
with

you.

Hold Me Tight

I yearn to be wrapped
in a passionate fiery love,
a warmth that seeps into my skin,
through my veins
and deep into my heart.

Values Of A Woman

Tenderness
I choose you,
love
here is my strength,
softness
what I nurture.

Enigma

Such quiet intensity,
the gaze in your eyes
how easily you seduced
me, it was hard to breathe
with fear
you'd see my weakness
that I only wanted

you.

I'm Your Angel

A myth and angel, you said
to me, I would be yours,
red lip stained kisses,
your addiction.

A shattered star,
raining dreams
you desire, my screams
piercing your soft, tender

soul.

Kintsugi

These feelings trickle
through the cracks of my heart and soul
aching to be filled,
for once,
        I don't want to be empty.

Pisces Sun

Come
in my warm waters,
stay,
pick your poison or your medicine,
this winter night,
in the deepest of abysses,
I will heal your soul

do not be afraid.

Moon In My Sky

You are my full moon falling,
waxing and waning,
deeper and deeper
into my cold and transparent heart.

You are my awakening touch,
see me with your delicate swaying eyes,
darker and darker
I merge with this night sky.

The One I Loved

His presence alone expanding
my heart in ways
I could barely reach.

His face
brings tears to my eyes,
slowly
spilling
down my cheeks,
rivers of silver.

His smile so radiant,
pure,
beautiful.

I was looking at an angel,
the fallen one

      who would come for my soul.

Unspoken Of

Loving you
was a twisted pleasure
I enjoyed deeply
even

if it hurt me.

Iron Heart

He was my inferno
seduced into hell
I burned, flesh and soul
and yet,
I wanted more.
I ran to him
with all my fury, all my love
embraced by his fires
melting in his heat

      finally feeling complete.

My Assassin Lover

I feared him
because I knew in an instant
he would become my reason
for breathing,
for living,
       and I did not know
how to embrace

such control
over me.

I Dwell In The Evenings

I could not be with someone
who cannot hold space
for my darkness,
because
it is in my darkness
that my light

        blooms in.

January 2021

You came to me
like spring
in the middle of winter,
and I realized the fragility
of my own heart
when I began to love you.

The way it blossomed,
petals unfurling,
discovering its own beauty
for the first time.

How easily you seeped
in through my veins, your soft
voice sung symphonies
to my ears.

The way your hands
left their imprints
on my tender skin.

You became
a part of me
and I
never wanted to let you

go.

The Gift You Gave Me

My oasis
of serenity amidst
the storms.
I found freedom
in your love

for me.

You set me free
and I spread my wings.

I soared,
feeling the sweet wind
on my face and body.

Yuanfen

The first man
who I felt could withstand
my tremendousness.
An extreme being, I am.
I drown
in depths,
that far more have run away
than those who dared
to stay.

I needed
one who would not be afraid
to dive in the water
to dance with on the ocean floor.
I wanted to be owned by him
but only if he proved
his effort and strength.

To make me desire to submit,

      that was his mission.

Springtime

Let me take you in my hand
hold you close to me,
your love is my oxygen
all I need to breathe

is you.

Because, I love you

I lost myself for a moment there
I did not know what to do,
but I believe in you,
and hope that one day, you will understand
the being I am.

My vulnerability and that I choose my softness
because I love you

oh,
how I love you.

Harsh Truth

Maybe my idea
of us
had grown so expansive,
the reality
could not keep up.

Invisibility

Do you see me? I ask,
I'm looking at you, you say.
I wept.
For the me you see
is only the version you desire me
to be
and who I am
had no space
to be free.

Tainted

I loved you
and I loved you deeply,
I loved you
with a naive innocence,
a sincere desperation,
yet you could not see,
made me out to be
the evil
in your story.

He Stole My Flowers

He walked into my heart
with no direction
lived there with no connection,
wilted my flowers,
spent my hours.

This Heartbreak

Deafening, the sound
of the shattering cracking of my heart
when it all

broke.

Piece by piece, falling
unable to hold myself together,
unwilling to let go
of what I thought was forever.

Unbearable
our bodies so close,
hearts

breaking
apart.

Turning The Page

I see your face one last time
and knew you were no longer mine,
it was clear to me,
this simply was not meant to be,
no regrets in the end

        through you
I am now ready to ascend.

Tragedies Of A Human's Life

There are days when familiar
places suddenly feel unfamiliar,
and when familiar faces
suddenly
become strangers.

Memory Of You

I remember
the way
it felt to be in your warm embrace,
a life we desired
to build together
you and I, we were meant to be forever.

But I, have realized some things never last
as much as I wish to relive our past,
it is not only the memories that are still alive,
I remember how you promised
to be by my side.

I remember
when you left
the way wind brushes against your skin,
how I wept and I wept
on my knees
I thought my heart
would never stop

breaking.

Bloody Tears

I have cried and bled
more than I can truly admit,
what I felt
for you, is my own punishment.

So I allowed myself to burn,
to fall,
feel the pain of losing it all,
the moment of true utter despair
freeing me,
of the mental and emotional chains
that bounded,
held against my will
I would no longer be ill.

Just like that, I let go of what I once held dear
instead of being filled with fear, my heart
and soul became lighter,
I learned in letting go
that some things are not meant to last forever.

In this state of being, I feel free,
once again my world of imagination
welcomed me, a place I find solace
a place for me that is lawless,
this very existence is a gift, I humbly
accept and enjoy simply
with a

perspective shift.

Absence

For reasons unknown
to me, I still yearned for you,
not realizing absence
itself,
becomes a presence too.

Feminine Urge

The more I understand, the more
I hurt, the more
I love, the more

I desire.

Lullaby

Sadness lingered
in my heart,
a misty fog that refused to leave.
Overtime the pain
becomes a comfortable ache
soon enough,
a lullaby
to lull you to sleep.

Unfulfilled

I wept
because I desired more
and more,
yet
to be fulfilled
in my yearning.

Back To The Beginning

Letting go of you
because it was time to hold
onto me, because I deserved
the same love
I gave so immensely to you.

Farewell

I will never be the same
and neither will you.
After all that we learned from our pain,
through all that we had to gain, to lose
in this life that we choose,
with our hearts
we have learned to use.

Reality

There are days I wake up and I miss my innocence.

The Last Petal To Fall

Some people pass
us by like seasons,
and though I wish to cling
on to the last bloom,
to preserve the last snow,
they eventually slip
away
because they know
        it is their time

to go.

Treasure Hunt

It was through
heartbreak
that I learned to love,
because of pain
I found my pleasure,
and in solitude,

       I find myself.

Birthing

In this moment, right now
I feel myself blossoming,
opening up.
I feel
the light within
bursting at my seams.

The deep desire
to express,
I can hardly contain it.

This feeling is so seductive,
calling my name
I close my eyes and I surrender.

In this moment, right now.

Contemplation

Overindulgent in escapism,
it is not easy to face
the difficult and painful,
however sooner or later, it will be time.
It is best to, sooner
          than later.

Change

The beauty of life
is the freedom
        of an ever-evolving self.
Still learning
who she is, what she wants.
Her hopes,
dreams,
wishes,
        how she desires
to move
within this world.

My Heart

I yearned
to be seen and heard,
it dawned on me
the necessity
to see,
to hear
            myself first.

To experience intimacy
            with my own heart.

My heart
I neglected for so long,
my heart
I abandoned,
my heart
            waiting
for me
to see, to hear

her.

Woman

I am more interested
in the woman
I want to be,
rather than, the things I want.
For by the time
          I am her,
I will have everything

I need.

Made In The Fine Details

Stay soft, my darling.

Your delicateness
does not mean you are weak,
it is in experiencing the tumultuous,
the tenderness,
undergoing fine workmanship
that intricacy is made.

Allow your soul,
heart,
and mind

to find their own beauty.

Forward

Renewed hope,
deeper sense of understanding,
a shift in perspectives.

Wisdom
reaped from pain,
to help me define.

Choosing to persist
in the unseen
because I now know
the power
of my being.

For this I will bloom,
because this is the only way

to move,
to live.

Life Philosophy

Wait for no one,
          but your own heart and soul.

Serenity

I closed my eyes and I was home.

The Tenderness Of Our Beauty

To embody my being,
to bloom in my becoming,
to remember who I am,
remembering

why

I began.

Returning

I may not know where my steps
may take me, I do know what my eyes
can see,
far beyond my senses,
       far beyond the horizon.

Will you dream

with me?

Reason To Exist

I hope in this lifetime,
you find what makes your heart
soar, the places and people
your heart beats for.
I promise
you, when we meet
my soul and your soul

at last will greet.

Lumen

I made love
to myself last night, opening
my eyes from my bliss
turning to the window
the bright full moon
gently blowing me a kiss
smiling,

how luminous
            she beamed.

Alethiology

You cannot find freedom
from your heart.

The Song I Sing To You Tonight

Drown me in your love
my rising sun, my evening moon
however fleeting
          you are immortal in my soul.

Thoughts Of My Twilight

Is anything forever
or just a fleeting feeling?

How strangely accurate
to describe anything and everything.
I shall pass through this life
touching upon moments
of pleasure, of pain.
Dancing my way through,
laughing and crying.

It'd be too sad to let this life be lived in vain.
No regrets, I tell myself.
But some days I can't tell,
where I'm going
or if I'm hiding.
Things can get blurry, but I always have hope

for clarity.

My Question To You

Because what is love,
without patience,
forgiveness
and the willingness

to grow?

Wherever you may be,
I hope you are filled with love.